Basics of Christianity

Basics of Christianity

By

Tracy Carol Taylor

The Basics of Christianity

Copyright © 2008 by Tracy Carol Taylor. All rights reserved.

This book or parts thereof may not be reproduced in any form, stored in a retrieval system or transmitted in any form by any means—electronic, mechanical, photocopy, recording or otherwise—without prior written permission of the publisher, except as provided by United States of America copyright law.

Unless otherwise noted, all Scripture quotations are from the Holy Bible copyright © 1989 by World Publishing, Iowa Falls, Iowa, 50126. All rights reserved.

Published by Prince of Pages, Inc.

N. Carlin Springs Road, Arlington, VA 22203

www.princeofpages.com

Published in United States of America

1. Religion, Christian Life, Devotional
2. Religion, Christian Life, Personal Growth

Cover Design by Getty Images

Contents

1. The Lord's Prayer ... 1
2. The 23rd Psalm ... 2
3. The Ten Commandants ... 3
4. The Old Testament ... 4
5. The New Testament ... 6
6. The B Attitudes ... 8
7. The 12 Disciples ... 10
8. The Plan of Salvation ... 11
9. Repentance: ... 23
10. Baptize: ... 24
11. Receive: ... 25
12. The Story of Nicodemus ... 26
13. The Fruits of the Spirit ... 29
14. The Getting and Keeping of Wisdom ... 31
15. The Godhead and/or The Trinity ... 39
16. The Armor of God ... 42
17. Legends of Lessons Learned ... 44
18. Bad Bad Bart ... 50

Other Books by Author

1. The Lord's Prayer

9 After this manner therefore pray ye: Our Father which art in heaven, Hallowed be thy name.

10 Thy kingdom come, Thy will be done in earth, as it is in heaven.

11 Give us this day our daily bread.

12 And forgive us our debts, as we forgive our debtors.

13 And lead us not into temptation, but deliver us from evil: For thine is the kingdom, and the power, and the glory, forever. Amen.

Matt 6:9-13 (KJV)

Lord's Prayer

2. The 23rd Psalm

1 The LORD is my shepherd; I shall not want.

2 He maketh me to lie down in green pastures: he leadeth me beside the still waters.

3 He restoreth my soul: he leadeth me in the paths of righteousness for his name's sake.

4 Yea, though I walk through the valley of the shadow of death, I will fear no evil: for thou art with me; thy rod and thy staff they comfort me.

5 Thou preparest a table before me in the presence of mine enemies: thou anointest my head with oil; my cup runneth over.

6 Surely goodness and mercy shall follow me all the days of my life: and I will dwell in the house of the LORD forever.

Psalm 23:1-6 (KJV)

3. The Ten Commandants

1. Thou shalt have no other gods before me.
2. Thou shalt not make unto thee any graven image.
3. Thou shalt not take the name of the LORD thy God in vain.
4. Remember the sabbath day, to keep it holy.
5. Honour thy father and thy mother.
6. Thou shalt not kill.
7. Thou shalt not commit adultery.
8. Thou shalt not steal.
9. Thou shalt not bear false witness against thy neighbour.
10. Thou shalt not covet thy neighbour's house; thou shalt not covet thy neighbour's wife, nor his manservant, nor his maidservant, nor his ox, nor his ass, nor any thing that is thy neighbour's.

Exodus 20:1-17 (KJV)

4. The Old Testament

Genesis
  Exodus
  Leviticus
  Numbers
  Deuteronomy
  Joshua
  Judges
  Ruth
  1 Samuel
  2 Samuel
  1 Kings
  2 Kings
  1 Chronicles
  2 Chronicles
  Ezra
  Nehemiah
  Esther
  Job
  Psalms
  Proverbs
  Ecclesiastes
  Song of Solomon
  Isaiah
  Jeremiah

Lamentations

Ezekiel

Daniel

Hosea

Joel

Amos

Obadiah

Jonah

Micah

Nahum

Habakkuk

Zephaniah

Haggai

Zechariah

Malachi

5. The New Testament

Matthew
  Mark
  Luke
  John
  Acts
  Romans
  1 Corinthians
  2 Corinthians
  Galatians
  Ephesians
  Philippians
  Colossians
  1 Thessalonians
  2 Thessalonians
  1Timothy
  2 Timothy
  Titus
  Philemon
  Hebrews
  James
  1 Peter
  2 Peter
  1 John
  2 John

3 John
Jude
Revelation

6. The B Attitudes

1 And seeing the multitudes, he went up into a mountain: and when he was set, his disciples came unto him:

2 And he opened his mouth, and taught them, saying,

3 Blessed are the poor in spirit: for theirs is the kingdom of heaven.

4 Blessed are they that mourn: for they shall be comforted.

5 Blessed are the meek: for they shall inherit the earth.

6 Blessed are they, which do hunger, and thirst after righteousness: for they shall be filled.

7 Blessed are the merciful: for they shall obtain mercy.

8 Blessed are the pure in heart: for they shall see God.

9 Blessed are the peacemakers: for they shall be called the children of God.

10 Blessed are they, which are persecuted for righteousness' sake: for theirs is the kingdom of heaven.

11 Blessed are ye, when men shall revile you, and persecute you, and shall say all manner of evil against you falsely, for my sake.

12 Rejoice, and be exceeding glad: for great is your reward in heaven: for so persecuted they the prophets which were before you.

13 Ye are the salt of the earth: but if the salt have lost his savour, wherewith shall it be salted? it is thenceforth good for nothing, but to be cast out, and to be trodden under foot of men.

14 Ye are the light of the world. A city that is set on an hill cannot be hid.

15 Neither do men light a candle, and put it under a bushel, but on a candlestick; and it giveth light unto all that are in the house.

16 Let your light so shine before men, that they may see your good works, and glorify your Father which is in heaven.

Matthew 5:1-11 (KJV)

7. The 12 Disciples

1. Peter
2. Andrew
3. James (son of Zebedee)
4. John (son of Zebedee)
5. Philip
6. Bartholomew
7. Thomas
8. Matthew (the Tax Collector)
9. James (son of Alphaeus)
10. Thaddaeus
11. Simon (the Zealot)
12. Judas Iscariot

Matthew 10:1-4 (KJV)

8. The Plan of Salvation

6 For unto us a child is born, unto us a son is given: and the government shall be upon his shoulder: and his name shall be called Wonderful, Counsellor, The mighty God, The everlasting Father, The Prince of Peace.

7 Of the increase of his government and peace there shall be no end, upon the throne of David, and upon his kingdom, to order it, and to establish it with judgment and with justice from henceforth even forever. The zeal of the Lord of hosts will perform this.

Isaiah 9:6-7 (KJV)

18 Now the birth of Jesus Christ was on this wise: When as his mother Mary was espoused to Joseph, before they came together, she was found with child of the Holy Ghost.

19 Then Joseph her husband, being a just man, and not willing to make her a public example, was minded to put her away privily.

20 But while he thought on these things, behold, the angel of the Lord appeared unto him in a dream, saying, Joseph, thou son of David, fear not to take unto thee Mary thy wife: for that which is conceived in her is of the Holy Ghost.

21 And she shall bring forth a son, and thou shalt call his name Jesus: for he shall save his people from their sins.

22 Now all this was done, that it might be fulfilled which was spoken of the Lord by the prophet, saying,

23 Behold, a virgin shall be with child, and shall bring forth a son, and they shall call his name Emmanuel, which being interpreted is, God with us.

Matthew 1:18-23 (KJV)

The Death of Jesus

15 Now at that feast the governor was wont to release unto the people a prisoner, whom they would.

16 And they had then a notable prisoner, called Barabbas.

17 Therefore when they were gathered together, Pilate said unto them, Whom will ye that I release unto you? Barabbas, or Jesus which is called Christ?

18 For he knew that for envy they had delivered him.

19 When he was set down on the judgment seat, his wife sent unto him, saying, Have thou nothing to do with that just man: for I have suffered many things this day in a dream because of him.

20 But the chief priests and elders persuaded the multitude that they should ask Barabbas, and destroy Jesus.

21 The governor answered and said unto them, Whether of the twain will ye that I release unto you? They said, Barabbas.

22 Pilate saith unto them, What shall I do then with Jesus which is called Christ? They all say unto him, Let him be crucified.

23 And the governor said, Why, what evil hath he done? But they cried out the more, saying, Let him be crucified.

24 When Pilate saw that he could prevail nothing, but that rather a tumult was made, he took water, and washed his hands before the multitude, saying, I am innocent of the blood of this just person: see ye to it.

25 Then answered all the people, and said, His blood be on us, and on our children.

26 Then released he Barabbas unto them: and when he had scourged Jesus, he delivered him to be crucified.

27 Then the soldiers of the governor took Jesus into the common hall, and gathered unto him the whole band of soldiers.

28 And they stripped him, and put on him a scarlet robe.

29 And when they had platted a crown of thorns, they put it upon his head, and a reed in his right hand: and they bowed the knee before him, and mocked him, saying, Hail, King of the Jews!

30 And they spit upon him, and took the reed, and smote him on the head.

31 And after that they had mocked him, they took the robe off from him, and put his own raiment on him, and led him away to crucify him.

32 And as they came out, they found a man of Cyrene, Simon by name: him they compelled to bear his cross.

33 And when they were come unto a place called Golgotha, that is to say, a place of a skull,

34 They gave him vinegar to drink mingled with gall: and when he had tasted thereof, he would not drink.

35 And they crucified him, and parted his garments, casting lots: that it might be fulfilled which was spoken by the prophet, They parted my garments among them, and upon my vesture did they cast lots.

36 And sitting down they watched him there;

37 And set up over his head his accusation written, This Is Jesus The King Of The Jews.

38 Then were there two thieves crucified with him, one on the right hand, and another on the left.

39 And they that passed by reviled him, wagging their heads,

40 And saying, Thou that destroyest the temple, and buildest it in three days, save thyself. If thou be the Son of God, come down from the cross.

41 Likewise also the chief priests mocking him, with the scribes and elders, said,

42 He saved others; himself he cannot save. If he be the King of Israel, let him now come down from the cross, and we will believe him.

43 He trusted in God; let him deliver him now, if he will have him: for he said, I am the Son of God.

44 The thieves also, which were crucified with him, cast the same in his teeth.

45 Now from the sixth hour there was darkness over all the land unto the ninth hour.

46 And about the ninth hour Jesus cried with a loud voice, saying, Eli, Eli, lama sabachthani? that is to say, My God, my God, why hast thou forsaken me?

47 Some of them that stood there, when they heard that, said, This man calleth for Elias.

48 And straightway one of them ran, and took a spunge, and filled it with vinegar, and put it on a reed, and gave him to drink.

49 The rest said, Let be, let us see whether Elias will come to save him.

50 Jesus, when he had cried again with a loud voice, yielded up the ghost.

51 And, behold, the veil of the temple was rent in twain from the top to the bottom; and the earth did quake, and the rocks rent;

52 And the graves were opened; and many bodies of the saints which slept arose,

53 And came out of the graves after his resurrection, and went into the holy city, and appeared unto many.

54 Now when the centurion, and they that were with him, watching Jesus, saw the earthquake, and those things that were done, they feared greatly, saying, Truly this was the Son of God.

Matthew 27:15-54 (KJV)

The Resurrection of Jesus Christ

1 Now upon the first day of the week, very early in the morning, they came unto the sepulcher, bringing the spices, which they had prepared, and certain others with them.

2 And they found the stone rolled away from the sepulcher.

3 And they entered in, and found not the body of the Lord Jesus.

4 And it came to pass, as they were much perplexed thereabout, behold, two men stood by them in shining garments:

5 And as they were afraid, and bowed down their faces to the earth, they said unto them, Why seek ye the living among the dead?

6 He is not here, but is risen: remember how he spake unto you when he was yet in Galilee,

7 Saying, The Son of man must be delivered into the hands of sinful men, and be crucified, and the third day rise again.

8 And they remembered his words,

9 And returned from the sepulcher, and told all these things unto the eleven, and to all the rest.

10 It was Mary Magdalene and Joanna, and Mary the mother of James, and other women that were with them, which told these things unto the apostles.

Luke 24:1-10 (KJV)

Jesus' Message for his Disciples

33 And they rose up the same hour, and returned to Jerusalem, and found the eleven gathered together, and them that were with them,

34 Saying, The Lord is risen indeed, and hath appeared to Simon.

35 And they told what things were done in the way, and how he was known of them in breaking of bread.

36 And as they thus spake, Jesus himself stood in the midst of them, and saith unto them, Peace be unto you.

37 But they were terrified and affrighted, and supposed that they had seen a spirit.

38 And he said unto them, Why are ye troubled? and why do thoughts arise in your hearts?

39 Behold my hands and my feet, that it is I myself: handle me, and see; for a spirit hath not flesh and bones, as ye see me have.

40 And when he had thus spoken, he shewed them his hands and his feet.

41 And while they yet believed not for joy, and wondered, he said unto them, Have ye here any meat?

42 And they gave him a piece of a broiled fish, and of an honeycomb.

43 And he took it, and did eat before them.

44 And he said unto them, These are the words which I spake unto you, while I was yet with you, that all things must be fulfilled, which were written in the law of Moses, and in the prophets, and in the psalms, concerning me.

45 Then opened he their understanding, that they might understand the scriptures,

46 And said unto them, Thus it is written, and thus it behooved Christ to suffer, and to rise from the dead the third day:

47 And that repentance and remission of sins should be preached in his name among all nations, beginning at Jerusalem.

48 And ye are witnesses of these things.

49 And, behold, I send the promise of my Father upon you: but tarry ye in the city of Jerusalem, until ye be endued with power from on high.

50 And he led them out as far as to Bethany, and he lifted up his hands, and blessed them.

51 And it came to pass, while he blessed them, he was parted from them, and carried up into heaven.

52 And they worshipped him, and returned to Jerusalem with great joy:

Luke 24:33-52 (KJV)

The Outpouring of the Holy Ghost

1 And when the day of Pentecost was fully come, they were all with one accord in one place.

2 And suddenly there came a sound from heaven as of a rushing mighty wind, and it filled all the house where they were sitting.

3 And there appeared unto them cloven tongues like as of fire, and it sat upon each of them.

4 And they were all filled with the Holy Ghost, and began to speak with other tongues, as the Spirit gave them utterance.

5 And there were dwelling at Jerusalem Jews, devout men, out of every nation under heaven.

6 Now when this was noised abroad, the multitude came together, and were confounded, because that every man heard them speak in his own language.

7 And they were all amazed and marvelled, saying one to another, Behold, are not all these which speak Galilaeans?

8 And how hear we every man in our own tongue, wherein we were born?

9 Parthians, and Medes, and Elamites, and the dwellers in Mesopotamia, and in Judaea, and Cappadocia, in Pontus, and Asia,

10 Phrygia, and Pamphylia, in Egypt, and in the parts of Libya about Cyrene, and strangers of Rome, Jews and proselytes,

11 Cretes and Arabians, we do hear them speak in our tongues the wonderful works of God.

12 And they were all amazed, and were in doubt, saying one to another, What meaneth this?

13 Others mocking said, These men are full of new wine.

14 But Peter, standing up with the eleven, lifted up his voice, and said unto them, Ye men of Judaea, and all ye that dwell at Jerusalem, be this known unto you, and hearken to my words:

15 For these are not drunken, as ye suppose, seeing it is but the third hour of the day.

16 But this is that which was spoken by the prophet Joel;

17 And it shall come to pass in the last days, saith God, I will pour out of my Spirit upon all flesh: and your sons and your daughters shall prophesy, and your young men shall see visions, and your old men shall dream dreams:

18 And on my servants and on my handmaidens I will pour out in those days of my Spirit; and they shall prophesy:

19 And I will shew wonders in heaven above, and signs in the earth beneath; blood, and fire, and vapour of smoke:

20 The sun shall be turned into darkness, and the moon into blood, before the great and notable day of the Lord come:

21 And it shall come to pass, that whosoever shall call on the name of the Lord shall be saved.

22 Ye men of Israel, hear these words; Jesus of Nazareth, a man approved of God among you by miracles and wonders and signs, which God did by him in the midst of you, as ye yourselves also know:

23 Him, being delivered by the determinate counsel

and foreknowledge of God, ye have taken, and by wicked hands have crucified and slain:

24 Whom God hath raised up, having loosed the pains of death: because it was not possible that he should be holden of it.

25 For David speaketh concerning him, I foresaw the Lord always before my face, for he is on my right hand, that I should not be moved:

26 Therefore did my heart rejoice, and my tongue was glad; moreover also my flesh shall rest in hope:

27 Because thou wilt not leave my soul in hell, neither wilt thou suffer thine Holy One to see corruption.

28 Thou hast made known to me the ways of life; thou shalt make me full of joy with thy countenance.

29 Men and brethren, let me freely speak unto you of the patriarch David, that he is both dead and buried, and his sepulchre is with us unto this day.

30 Therefore being a prophet, and knowing that God had sworn with an oath to him, that of the fruit of his loins, according to the flesh, he would raise up Christ to sit on his throne;

31 He seeing this before spake of the resurrection of Christ, that his soul was not left in hell, neither his flesh did see corruption.

32 This Jesus hath God raised up, whereof we all are witnesses.

33 Therefore being by the right hand of God exalted, and having received of the Father the promise of the Holy

Ghost, he hath shed forth this, which ye now see and hear.

34 For David is not ascended into the heavens: but he saith himself, The Lord said unto my Lord, Sit thou on my right hand,

35 Until I make thy foes thy footstool.

36 Therefore let all the house of Israel know assuredly, that God hath made the same Jesus, whom ye have crucified, both Lord and Christ.

37 Now when they heard this, they were pricked in their heart, and said unto Peter and to the rest of the apostles, Men and brethren, what shall we do?

38 Then Peter said unto them, Repent, and be baptized every one of you in the name of Jesus Christ for the remission of sins, and ye shall receive the gift of the Holy Ghost.

39 For the promise is unto you, and to your children, and to all that are afar off, even as many as the LORD our God shall call.

40 And with many other words did he testify and exhort, saying, save yourselves from this untoward generation.

41 Then they that gladly received his word were baptized: and the same day there were added unto them about three thousand souls.

Acts 2:1-41 (KJV)

9. Repentance:

The action or process of feeling regret or contrition especially for misdeeds or moral shortcomings; To turn from sin and dedicate oneself to the amendment of one's life.

10. Baptize:

To purify or cleanse spiritually especially by a purging experience.

11. Receive:

To come into possession of...i.e. a gift or present.

12. The Story of Nicodemus

1 There was a man of the Pharisees, named Nicodemus, a ruler of the Jews:

2 The same came to Jesus by night, and said unto him, Rabbi, we know that thou art a teacher come from God: for no man can do these miracles that thou doest, except God be with him.

3 Jesus answered and said unto him, Verily, verily, I say unto thee, Except a man be born again, he cannot see the kingdom of God.

4 Nicodemus saith unto him, How can a man be born when he is old? can he enter the second time into his mother's womb, and be born?

5 Jesus answered, Verily, verily, I say unto thee, Except a man be born of water and of the Spirit, he cannot enter into the kingdom of God.

6 That which is born of the flesh is flesh; and that which is born of the Spirit is spirit.

7 Marvel not that I said unto thee, Ye must be born again.

8 The wind bloweth where it listeth, and thou hearest the sound thereof, but canst not tell whence it cometh, and whither it goeth: so is every one that is born of the Spirit.

9 Nicodemus answered and said unto him, How can these things be?

10 Jesus answered and said unto him, Art thou a master of Israel, and knowest not these things?

11 Verily, verily, I say unto thee, We speak that we do know, and testify that we have seen; and ye receive not our witness.

12 If I have told you earthly things, and ye believe not, how shall ye believe, if I tell you of heavenly things?

13 And no man hath ascended up to heaven, but he that came down from heaven, even the Son of man which is in heaven.

14 And as Moses lifted up the serpent in the wilderness, even so must the Son of man be lifted up:

15 That whosoever believeth in him should not perish, but have eternal life.

16 For God so loved the world, that he gave his only begotten Son, that whosoever believeth in him should not perish, but have everlasting life.

17 For God sent not his Son into the world to condemn the world; but that the world through him might be saved.

18 He that believeth on him is not condemned: but he that believeth not is condemned already, because he hath not believed in the name of the only begotten Son of God.

19 And this is the condemnation, that light is come

into the world, and men loved darkness rather than light, because their deeds were evil.

20 For every one that doeth evil hateth the light, neither cometh to the light, lest his deeds should be reproved.

21 But he that doeth truth cometh to the light that his deeds may be made manifest, that they are wrought in God.

22 After these things came Jesus and his disciples into the land of Judaea; and there he tarried with them, and baptized.

23 And John also was baptizing in Aenon near to Salim, because there was much water there: and they came, and were baptized.

John 3:1-23 (KJV)

13. The Fruits of the Spirit

22 But the fruit of the Spirit is love, joy, peace, patience, kindness, goodness, faithfulness,

23 gentleness and self-control. Against such things there is no law.

Galatians 5:22-23 (KJV)

Definitions of:

1. Love: a profoundly tender, passionate affection for another person.
2. Joy: the emotion of great delight or happiness caused by something exceptionally good.
3. Peace: a state of mutual harmony between people or groups.
4. Patience: an ability or willingness to suppress restlessness or annoyance when confronted with delay.
5. Kindness: the quality of being warmhearted and considerate and humane and sympathetic.
6. Goodness: that which is pleasing or valuable or useful, morally excellent or admirable.
7. Faithfulness: Adhering firmly and devotedly, as to a

person, cause, or idea; loyal.
8. Gentleness: Considerate or kindly in disposition; amiable and tender.
9. Self-Control: Control of one's emotions, desires, or actions by one's own will.

14. The Getting and Keeping of Wisdom

A Manual for Living
(from the New International Version Bible)

Proverbs: The Wise Sayings of King Solomon

1 The proverbs of Solomon son of David, king of Israel:

2 for attaining wisdom and discipline; for understanding words of insight;

3 for acquiring a disciplined and prudent life, doing what is right and just and fair;

4 for giving prudence to the simple, knowledge and discretion to the young-

5 let the wise listen and add to their learning, and let the discerning get guidance-

6 for understanding proverbs and parables, the sayings and riddles of the wise.

7 The fear of the LORD is the beginning of knowledge, but fools despise wisdom and discipline.

8 Listen, my son, to your father's instruction and do not forsake your mother's teaching.

9 They will be a garland to grace your head and a chain to adorn your neck.

10 My son, if sinners entice you, do not give in to them.

11 If they say, "Come along with us; let's lie in wait for someone's blood, let's waylay some harmless soul;

12 let's swallow them alive, like the grave, and whole, like those who go down to the pit;

13 we will get all sorts of valuable things and fill our houses with plunder;

14 throw in your lot with us, and we will share a common purse"-

15 my son, do not go along with them, do not set foot on their paths;

16 for their feet rush into sin, they are swift to shed blood.

17 How useless to spread a net in full view of all the birds!

18 These men lie in wait for their own blood; they waylay only themselves!

19 Such is the end of all who go after ill-gotten gain; it takes away the lives of those who get it.

Proverbs 1:1-19 (NIV)

The Benefits of Wisdom

1 My son, if you accept my words and store up my commands within you,

2 turning your ear to wisdom and applying your heart to understanding,

3 and if you call out for insight and cry aloud for understanding,

4 and if you look for it as for silver and search for it as for hidden treasure,

5 then you will understand the fear of the LORD and find the knowledge of God.

6 For the LORD gives wisdom, and from his mouth come knowledge and understanding.

7 He holds victory in store for the upright, he is a shield to those whose walk is blameless,

8 for he guards the course of the just and protects the way of his faithful ones.

9 Then you will understand what is right and just and fair—every good path.

10 For wisdom will enter your heart, and knowledge will be pleasant to your soul.

11 Discretion will protect you, and understanding will guard you.

12 Wisdom will save you from the ways of wicked men, from men whose words are perverse,

13 who leave the straight paths to walk in dark ways,

14 who delight in doing wrong and rejoice in the perverseness of evil,

15 whose paths are crooked and who are devious in their ways.

Proverbs 2:1-15 (NIV)

Do not fear discipline and rebuke, they will make you a better person.

1 My son, do not forget my teaching, but keep my commands in your heart,

2 for they will prolong your life many years and bring you prosperity.

3 Let love and faithfulness never leave you; bind them around your neck, write them on the tablet of your heart.

4 Then you will win favor and a good name in the sight of God and man.

5 Trust in the LORD with all your heart and lean not on your own understanding;

6 in all your ways acknowledge him, and he will make your paths straight.

7 Do not be wise in your own eyes; fear the LORD and shun evil.

8 This will bring health to your body and nourishment to your bones.

9 Honor the LORD with your wealth, with the firstfruits of all your crops;

10 then your barns will be filled to overflowing, and your vats will brim over with new wine.

11 My son, do not despise the Lord's discipline and do not resent his rebuke,

12 because the LORD disciplines those he loves, as a father the son he delights in.

Proverbs 3:1-12 (NIV)

27 Do not withhold good from those who deserve it, when it is in your power to act.

28 Do not say to your neighbor, "Come back later; I'll give it tomorrow" when you now have it with you.

29 Do not plot harm against your neighbor, who lives trustfully near you.

30 Do not accuse a man for no reason, when he has done you no harm.

31 Do not envy a violent man or choose any of his ways,

32 for the LORD detests a perverse man but takes the upright into his confidence.

Proverbs 3:27-32 (NIV)

Do not follow what bad men say or do.

10 Listen, my son, accept what I say, and the years of your life will be many.

11 I guide you in the way of wisdom and lead you along straight paths.

12 When you walk, your steps will not be hampered; when you run, you will not stumble.

13 Hold on to instruction, do not let it go; guard it well, for it is your life.

14 Do not set foot on the path of the wicked or walk in the way of evil men.

15 Avoid it, do not travel on it; turn from it and go on your way.

16 For they cannot sleep till they do evil; they are robbed of slumber till they make someone fall.

17 They eat the bread of wickedness and drink the wine of violence.

18 The path of the righteous is like the first gleam of dawn, shining ever brighter till the full light of day.

Proverbs 4:10-18 (NIV)

24 Put away perversity from your mouth; keep corrupt talk far from your lips.

25 Let your eyes look straight ahead, fix your gaze directly before you.

26 Make level paths for your feet and take only ways that are firm.

27 Do not swerve to the right or the left; keep your foot from evil.

Proverbs 4:24-27 (NIV)

Don't be lazy or silly with your ways.

6 Go to the ant, you sluggard; consider its ways and be wise!

7 It has no commander, no overseer or ruler,

8 yet it stores its provisions in summer and gathers its food at harvest.

9 How long will you lie there, you sluggard? When will you get up from your sleep?

10 A little sleep, a little slumber, a little folding of the hands to rest-

11 and poverty will come on you like a bandit and scarcity like an armed man.

12 A scoundrel and villain, who goes about with a corrupt mouth,

13 who winks with his eye, signals with his feet and motions with his fingers,

14 who plots evil with deceit in his heart, he always stirs up dissension.

15 Therefore disaster will overtake him in an instant; he will suddenly be destroyed, without remedy.

16 There are six things the LORD hates, seven that are detestable to him:

17 haughty eyes, a lying tongue, hands that shed innocent blood,

18 a heart that devises wicked schemes, feet that are quick to rush into evil,

19 a false witness who pours out lies and a man who stirs up dissension among brothers.

Proverbs 6:6-19 (NIV)

Remember the greatest commandment:

36 "Teacher, which is the greatest commandment in the Law?"

37 Jesus replied: "Love the Lord your God with all your heart and with all your soul and with all your mind."

38 This is the first and greatest commandment.

39 And the second is like it: 'Love your neighbor as yourself.'

40 All the Law and the Prophets hang on these two commandments."

Matthew 22:36-40 (NIV)

In other words: do unto others as you would have them do unto you. If you want good things to happen to you, then do good things for others. And if you're a techie: Garbage in = Garbage out. Nothing good will happen to you, if you are always doing bad things to others.

15. The Godhead and/or The Trinity

The mystery of the Father, the Son, and the Holy Ghost has always tended to stump people; especially, when Jesus himself used to pray to God the father. People never could understand how one could pray to himself. And this is the way that it was explained to me.

Water has three forms, but it is still water. Water becomes ice when it is cold enough and it becomes steam when it is hot enough. So if God is water, then when he became a man and became Jesus Christ, he was water becoming ice. When Jesus Christ died on the cross and ascended to heaven, he became the Holy Ghost; water becoming steam.

Or think of it this way, if a man can be a grandfather, a father, and a son and still be the same person; then why can't God, who is all powerful and all knowing.

Or better yet...Have you ever talked to yourself?

Now we know that Jesus was God's human form in the flesh. But if you read Genesis 3:8, then you know that...

"**8** And they heard the voice of the Lord God walking in the garden in the cool of the day: and Adam and his wife hid themselves from the presence of the Lord God amongst the trees of the garden."

So we know that whether in the Old Testament or in the New Testament, the Lord God Jesus Christ walks among his people.

"Yet for us there is but one God, the Father, from whom all things came and for whom we live; and there is but one Lord, Jesus Christ, through whom all things came and through whom we live."

1 Corinthians 8:6 (NIV)

"One God and Father of all, who is over all and through all and in all."

Ephesians 4:6 (KJV)

Jesus answered: "Don't you know me, Philip, even after I have been among you such a long time? Anyone who has seen me has seen the Father. How can you say, 'Show us the Father'?"

John 14:9 (NIV)

Hear, O Israel: The LORD our God, the LORD is one.
Deuteronomy 6:4 (NIV)

Final thought: The Trinity of The Godhead is really no mystery when you know that Jesus never did anything without a reason. Everything he did was an example to us. Whether it was how to pray, how to be baptized, or how to treat others. Jesus was always showing us what to do by example. So by praying to God the Father, he was showing us what to do even in the most stressful of situations. By allowing himself to be baptized by John the Baptist, he was showing us that submersion is the only way to be baptized. By washing the feet of his disciples, he was showing us service to others.

Finally, so that people couldn't say later "well, Jesus didn't have to do it, so why should I have to do it?"

16. The Armor of God

10 Finally, be strong in the Lord and in his mighty power.

11 Put on the full armor of God so that you can take your stand against the devil's schemes.

12 For our struggle is not against flesh and blood, but against the rulers, against the authorities, against the powers of this dark world and against the spiritual forces of evil in the heavenly realms.

13 Therefore put on the full armor of God, so that when the day of evil comes, you may be able to stand your ground, and after you have done everything, to stand.

14 Stand firm then, with the belt of truth buckled around your waist, with the breastplate of righteousness in place,

15 and with your feet fitted with the readiness that comes from the gospel of peace.

16 In addition to all this, take up the shield of faith, with which you can extinguish all the flaming arrows of the evil one.

17 Take the helmet of salvation and the sword of the Spirit, which is the word of God.

18 And pray in the Spirit on all occasions with all kinds of prayers and requests. With this in mind, be alert and always keep on praying for all the saints.

Ephesians 6:10-18 (NIV)

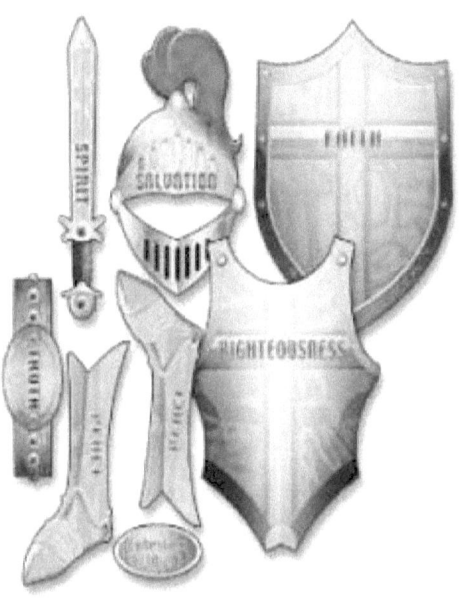

17. Legends of Lessons Learned

The Treasure Hunt

Its summertime and school is out. Betty and Bobby wanted to have some fun.

"I know." said Bobby. "Mr. Thompson from the general store is having a treasure hunt."

"He is?" said Betty, with great surprise.

"Yep. Want to play?" asked Bobby.

"Yes." said Betty.

So Betty and Bobby went to Mr. Thompson's to join in the Treasure hunt. There were lots of kids there. Soon Mr. Thompson came and handed out the lists.

"Here is a list of all the things that I want you to bring back here. Okay, off you go!" said Mr. Thompson.

All the kids ran off in all directions. Bobby and Betty also ran off to find their things. First on the list was a shovel.

Bobby found one in Mr. Brown yard.

"Hey, Mr. Brown can I have your shovel for my treasure hunt?" asked Bobby.

"You mean Mr. Thompson is having another hunt?" asked Mr. Brown.

"Yes, now can I have you shovel?" asked Bobby.

"I'm sorry Bobby, but I need it." said Mr. Brown.

"But I need it more." whined Bobby.

"But I have work to do." said Mr. Brown.

"Fine." said Bobby, angrily.

Bobby waited until Mr. Brown went inside for some water, and then he stole Mr. Brown's shovel.

Betty found her shovel in Mr. Tim's yard.

"Hi, Mr. Tim." smiled Betty.

"Hi Betty." smiled Mr. Tim.

"Mr. Tim can I borrow your shovel for Mr. Thompson's Treasure hunt?" asked Betty.

"Sorry Betty, I've got a hole to dig. I need it." said Mr. Tim.

"What if I help you dig the trench, then can I borrow your shovel?" asked Betty.

"Sure, but I only have one shovel." said Mr. Tim.

"I can take away the dirt in the wheel barrow and I can make sandwiches." offered Betty.

"Deal." smiled Mr. Tim.

An hour later, Mr. Tim finished the hole. He thanked Betty for her help and gave her the shovel.

The next item on the list was an apple pie.

Bobby found an apple pie sitting on Mrs. Williams' window.

"Hey Mrs. Williams." said Bobby.

"Oh, Hello Bobby." smiled Mrs. Williams.

"I'm in a treasure hunt, can I have your apple pie?" asked Bobby.

"No, Bobby this apple pie is for my son James. He comes home from the Army today. I made this pie just for him." said Mrs. Williams, proudly.

"But I need this pie for Mr. Thompson's treasure hunt." whined Bobby.

"I'm sorry Bobby." said Mrs. Williams.

Just then the doorbell rang.

"That must be James now." said Mrs. Williams.

Mrs. Williams left to answer the door.

"Sorry Mrs. Williams, but I need this pie more than you do. Take your son out to dinner why don't you." thought Bobby.

And then Bobby stole the apple pie.

Betty found her pie on Mrs. Jenson's window.

"Hello, Mrs. Jenson?" called Betty.

But she got no answer.

"Hm, no one's here. I could take the pie, but that would be stealing. I guess I could make a pie. But I don't know how." reasoned Betty.

"Oh, Betty, what are you doing here?" asked Mrs. Jenson.

"Oh, there you are. I came to ask if I can take your pie for Mr. Thompson's Treasure hunt." said Betty.

"I'd like to help you Betty, but I need this pie for desert." said Mrs. Jenson.

"That's alright. I'd rather you teach me to make pies for myself." said Betty.

"Oh, that's a good idea." agreed Mrs. Jenson.

So Mrs. Jenson taught Betty to make apple pies, and an hour later, Betty had her apple pie.

There were many other things on the list, and Betty and Bobby collected as many as they could.

Finally, Mr. Thompson announced the winner of the Treasure Hunt.

"The Winner of the treasure hunt is ... Betty." announced Mr. Thompson.

"Wait a minute." said Bobby. "I got more stuff than she did, and she was the last one back. Why did she win?"

"She won because not only did she bring stuff back, but she brought back treasure." said Mr. Thompson.

"What treasure?" asked Bobby. "She got the same stuff I did."

"She helped Mr. Tim dig his hole and gained his respect. She learned how to bake pies from Mrs. Jenson and gained knowledge." said Mr. Thompson. "Not all treasure is stuff Bobby. Some treasures are the friends we make or the knowledge we gain."

"That's just stupid." pouted Bobby.

Bobby had really wanted to win.

"Now Bobby, about all the things you stole." said Mr. Thompson. "Not only will you have to give them back, but you will work one hour for each person that you stole from."

"But I asked them first, they said no." cried Bobby.

"Then you should have found another way." said Mr. Thompson. "We should always treat other people as we would like to be treated. I assume you don't want anyone stealing your favorite bike."

"No way." said Bobby.

"Then how do you think they felt when you stole their stuff." said Mr. Thompson.

"You're right. I'm sorry." said Bobby.

"Don't apologized to me." said Mr. Thompson. "Go apologize to the people that you stole from."

"Okay." said Bobby. "Congratulations on winning the Treasure hunt Betty."

"Thank you Bobby." said Betty. "Do you want some of my Apple Pie?"

"Wow, you bet." said Bobby. "You really made this pie."

"Yes." smiled Betty. "I did."

Bobby apologized to Mr. Williams and Mr. Brown and some others. It took Bobby a while to work of his debt to society, but he did. At the end of the day, he and Betty enjoyed her Apple Pie with Vanilla ice cream. And Bobby learned that it was better to be a good friend than to have all the stuff in the world.

What do you consider to be treasure?

Is it your friends, your family, or something special that was given to you? Not all Treasure is silver and gold; but the knowledge we learn and the love of friends that we share.

18. Bad Bad Bart

Once upon a time, there was a little boy named Bart. He was a mean and nasty little boy. He played mean tricks on people. He'd steal from people and he always beat up kids smaller than him.

Now, there was also a little girl named Kimi. She was good, smart, and kind others. And she believed in the golden rule. "Do to others as you would have them do to you."

That means if you don't want your stuff stolen, then don't steal from others. If you don't want to get beat up, then don't beat up others. Always treat people the way you want to be treated. (that includes your brothers and sister, whether you like them or not).

One day, it was raining outside. I mean really really raining. Bart looked at the rain and groaned.

"Man, I don't want to get wet." said Bart. "I'll need an umbrella."

So Bart waited for the next kid to pass by and Bart stole his umbrella.

"But if you take my umbrella." cried the little boy. "How will I get home?"

"Who cares what happens to you." said Bart. "So long as I don't get wet."

Bart laughed as he pushed the little boy out into the

rain. Bart laughed as he walked home with the little boy's umbrella. The little boy hurried back into the school and out of the rain. Then he began to cry as he watched the rain fall.

Just then, Kimi walked by. She heard the little boy crying and stopped to see if she could help.

"Why are you crying?" asked Kimi.

"That mean boy, Bart, stole my umbrella. And he pushed me down in the rain. Now how will I get home." he cried. "My mom will be mad at me if I come home without my umbrella."

"Don't cry. You can have my umbrella." smiled Kimi.

"Really? But how will you get home?" asked the little boy.

"It's okay. I'll just call my dad. He'll pick me up." said Kimi.

"Thanks Kimi. You're really nice." smiled the little boy.

"You're welcome."

The little boy gave Kimi a hug, took the umbrella, and ran home.

The next day, Kimi caught Bart beating up another little boy for his lunch money.

"Stop that!" shouted Kimi. "Why are you beating him up?"

"Because I can." laughed Bart. "Besides he owes me money."

"Here take it." cried the little boy. "Just leave me alone!"

Bart took the money and let the boy go. Bart smiled.

"Alright, now I've got enough money for a new comic book."

Kimi frowned at Bart.

"You shouldn't do that to people." said Kimi.

"And why not?" asked Bart.

"You wouldn't want people doing it to you, would you?" asked Kimi.

"Like anyone would dare challenge me." laughed Bart.

"Bart, you can't…" began Kimi.

"Aw, save your preaching for Sunday school. I don't care." said Bart.

Bart walked away, whistling to himself. Kimi watched him go with sadness in her eyes. She knew that one day his evil deeds would haunt him.

It was Friday, the last day of school before summer vacation. Bart was looking forward to having fun. He planned to go to the movies, go swimming, and to go skateboarding. Yes, he had a fun filled summer planned. But then something happened that he hadn't planned on. Three big kids from high school ganged up on him.

"Who are you and what do you want?" asked Bart.

"I'm Tom. You stole my little brother's umbrella." said Tom.

"I'm Jimmy. You stole my little brother's lunch money." said Jimmy.

"And I'm Kevin. You beat up my little brother just because you could." said Kevin.

"So now, we're going to beat you up." said Tom.

"Why? Just because we can." said Jimmy.

Bart got scared and Bart ran. He didn't know that the kids he had picked on had older brothers. Bart ran and ran, but he couldn't outrun them. They three big boys caught up to Bart and beat Bart up. Bart screamed and cried for help, but no one came. Bart wanted them to stop, but they wouldn't. Then Bart thought about Kimi. She had told him that one day his evil deeds would catch up to him and today was that day. Bart screamed in pain as Jimmy broke his arm.

"OWWW!" cried Bart.

"That's enough Jimmy." said Kevin.

"Yeah, he won't pick on anybody else ever again." said Tom. "Right, Bart."

"Yeah, yeah." cried Bart. "Never again."

"Promise?" asked Kevin, making a fist.

"I promise." shouted Bart, in fear.

"Come on guys. Let's go." said Tom.

"Just a minute." said Jimmy. "Come on Bart, cough it up."

"Cough up what?" asked Bart.

"All the money in your pockets." said Jimmy.

"But how will I get home?" asked Bart.

"Who cares." said Tom.

The three big boys left, and Bart sat there crying. He was in pain and his arm was broken. Suddenly, he heard the voices of girls. Just then, Kimi and her friends were passing by. They were going to the mall to watch the latest movie. Bart called out to them.

"Kimi." called Bart. "I need your help."

Kimi stopped and looked at Bart.

"What happened to you?" she asked.

"I got beat up." Bart said, sadly.

"Hey Kimi, what are you doing?" asked Sally.

"He needs help. Someone beat him up." said Kimi.

"That's Bart." said Amy. "I'm not helping him.

"Yeah, he's so mean that everyone calls him Bad Bart." said Sally.

Bart frowned. They were right. He was mean. Why should they help him? Bart hung his head and walked away.

"Well, if you were hurt and alone, wouldn't you want someone to help you." said Kimi. "Bart wait."

"Yeah, I guess I would." said Amy.

"You guys go on ahead. I catch up later." said Kimi.

The girls walked away. Bart heard them laugh at him as they walked away.

"So Bad Bart finally got what he deserves." they laughed.

Bart felt bad. He couldn't look Kimi in the eye. He just watched in silence as Kimi cleaned up his wounds and bandaged his broken arm.

"Where'd you learn to do that?" asked Bart.

"From my dad." said Kimi. "He's a doctor."

"Thanks Kimi." said Bart, shyly. "Thanks for helping me."

"You're welcome." said Kimi. "But your arm is broken, so come on and see my dad. He'll fix your arm up."

Kimi walked with Bart to her father's doctor's office.

"Why are you helping me?" asked Bart. "After what I've done, I wouldn't help me."

"Bart, it's like I said. Do to others as you would have them do to you." said Kimi.

Bart smiled at Kimi.

"You were right, Kimi." said Bart. "I should have listened to you. Okay, you can say it."

"Say what?" asked Kimi.

"I told you so." said Bart.

"I told you so." smiled Kimi.

Kimi's father put Bart's arm in a cast. With this cast, Bart's fun filled summer was ruined. He couldn't go swimming, or ride his bike or play ball. He would have spent his whole summer in the house moping, if it weren't for Kimi.

Kimi came to see him almost every day. It made him happy that Kimi came to see him. And after that, they were the best of friends. Bart stopped doing bad things and he started to do good things. With Kimi's help, Bart learned to share. He learned to care for others, and he learned that helping other people actually made him feel good. Bart and Kimi not only spent the summer going to the movies, but they helped tutor the kids that had to go to summer school.

By the time school started again, Bart and Kimi had lots of friends. And the kids no longer called Bart, Bad Bart. They started calling him Blessed Bart. Bart even apologized to all the kids he used to beat up. One day, Bart got a surprise.

"Hey Bart, my dad owns an amusement park." said Jon. "You want to come."

"I remember you. Your Jon, I stole your umbrella and your brother Tom beat me up." said Bart. "Why would you want to invite me to your father's amusement park?"

"Because you and Kimi helped me pass summer school math." said Jon. "So you and Kimi want to come?"

"You bet." said Bart. "Thanks Jon."

So Bart called Kimi and he and Kimi and Jon and Tom all went to the amusement part. And they all had a great time, together.

60 Christian Traits
   The Basics of Christianity
   Cavities of the Caribbean
   The Journey
   Small Fry Tales
   Tale of Two Teeth
   Toothache at Big Mouth Bend
   Wondering Ardor
   Your Dental ABCs

   www.princeofpages.com

www.ingramcontent.com/pod-product-compliance
Lightning Source LLC
Chambersburg PA
CBHW020628300426
44112CB00010B/1234